Sky and Island Light

poems by Brendan Galvin

LOUISIANA STATE
UNIVERSITY PRESS
Baton Rouge and London
1996

Manufactured in the United States of America
First printing
05 04 03 02 01 00 99 98 97 96 1 2 3 4 5

Designer: Amanda McDonald Key
Typeface: Sabon
Typesetter: Impressions Book and Journal Services, Inc.
Printer and binder: Thomson-Shore, Inc.

LIBRARY OF CONGRESS CATALOGING-IN-PUBLICATION DATA

Galvin, Brendan.
Sky and island light : poems / by Brendan Galvin.
p. cm.
ISBN 0-8071-2108-8 (cl : alk. paper). — ISBN 0-8071-2109-6 (p : alk. paper)
I. Title.
PS3557.A44S58 1997
811'.54—dc20 96-30203
CIP

The author thanks the editors of the following periodicals, in which these poems originally appeared, sometimes in slightly different form: *Atlantic Monthly, Black Warrior Review, Colorado Review, Georgia Review, Gettysburg Review, Kenyon Review, Modern Age, New Criterion, New Review, Northeast, Poetry, Prairie Schooner, Shenandoah,* and *Tar River Poetry*. "The Patience of White Birches" originally appeared in *The New Yorker*. "Anchorites," "Crossing Pentland Firth," "Far Mulliskay," "Norwegians at the Shetland Hotel," "Sky and Island Light," "The Stones of Callanish," "Under My Stornoway Hat," and "West Cork: The Road Bowlers" appeared in *Islands*, a chapbook hand-printed in 1993 in an edition of a hundred on handmade paper at the Center for Book Arts, University of Alabama, under the direction of Paula M. Gourley.

The author also offers thanks to the John Simon Guggenheim Memorial Foundation and the National Endowment for the Arts for fellowships that enabled him to write many of the poems, to Connecticut State University for research grants, and to the School of Arts and Sciences, Central Connecticut State University, for support in the form of released time for research.

The paper in this book meets the guidelines for permanence and durability of the Committee on Production Guidelines for Book Longevity of the Council on Library Resources. ♾

for Owen Galvin

Contents

Sky and Island Light

Skylights

Every October, after a day when something
exotic has landed at the feeder
and waits gasping there as on a prow
far out at sea, a myrtle or Canada warbler
just too wing-beaten to go on,
I wake late to a good dinner
building its cloud above my heart,
and look up where stars in the skylight
on that night alone have a connect-the-dots
logic, a plan I might follow that's pressing
like a template in my head. Then I envision
the great streaming freeways of the birds,
those swerves and swoopings in every
color of feather, three miles up, blurred
Crayola streaks a hemisphere long, and
Surinam, French Guiana, Venezuela
loom in a summer down there
like the eminence of a new green heart.
I play around with gravity and magnetic
lines of force trined with the pull of the moon,
but panic hearing the surf of a different
coast in each ear, and drop to name
real hills instead: Tom's and Cathedral
enfolding an arm of river between
bay and ocean; Round and Corn, between
the freshwater lens my pump taps into
and those stars. Husband, father to sleepers,
doorman to dogs, I can't convert pasta
to vector energy anyway. I might say
something I ate causes this,
and tip an invisible nightcap
to the birds, who know where they're going
and how to get there.

A Ring of Quail Bones

I found them just off the fireroad
by the marsh, around a low
bush of wind-stripped sweet gale,
breastbones like ploughshares,
skulls papery, still unscuffled where
they'd crouched in their circle,
heads outward, still facing
whatever night brings, ready
to explode up the air
that found them out and feathered them
a flake at a time and left them under
rain and crust. This morning,
my gaze drawn upward by a muffled
thump at the skylight, three
drank on yellow feet
from a gathered night rain,
their bellies patterned with arrowheads,
another little drama of the fall;
and certain gifts from childhood
occurred, models of perfection I had
no fingers fine enough to assemble.

Nimblejacks

Remember Hot Spats and the Kaiser,
who illustrated the beautiful
moving-while-standing-still word
nimblejack, a word worthy of
a class of sailboats, like sneakbox,
or sharpie? I'm talking soupbeards
and rent-laggards like Boofer,
who checked out the coinbox on every
payphone in town. I'm talking
skewfooted Dr. Highpockets, who'd share
the sandwich in his carrot bag with anyone.
When was the last time Pungie
yawped at you across the street to say
how well that new puddle was doing
on the wrong side of the dike?
How about Tick, and the Man of Steel,
walk-ons from normality's hinterland,
part of the 9 percent who never have an opinion?
They were the canaries in our mineshaft,
our early warning systems, and never
disappeared into the shops all day,
but stayed on the sidewalks to hinder
the broom of the future simply by being there.
Not one ever asked, "Are you affiliated
with any academic institution?"
or propped Einstein's essays
strategically in a window of the Land Rover,
but remember how they used to line us up
in their sights on Main Street,
leaning left and right to keep us level?

Cobwebs on the Hillside

You could explain it away
as the house bracing
for sea fog laid against it,
but I woke to oarlocks
and the creaking
of a wooden boat, then
footsteps I could follow
by ear from tree to tree.
Only mist dripping
off branches, maybe,
though all night
I overheard the music of
flirtation out there,
harmonies fitted to each other
as you and I curl
together in sleep.
The hill dreaming its dead
up again, its happy isle
of Atwoods and Snows,
Dyers and Smalls
we know vestigially:
a wild roadside asparagus
fern, a wormed cedar
fencepost the barn swallows
have stuffed with mud
and straw. Before coffee
and sense take hold, look
out at these sheet webs
the spiders make and fog
lifts into sight, these
napkins of some long-ago
breakfast in the grass.

Draggers

When nothing's going on but wind
and every street's a back street,
I love to drive among white
clapboard houses that seem huddled
to the road in this short light,
and between the empty gallerias
which, come April, will change
names again.

Origins II, formerly Lobelia
Handcrafts, will become Something
Else, sure as the sign
in the closed chromium fishmarket
reads Strawberry Bass because
few anymore will eat a thing
called tautog.

Needing the romance of a
steepled seaside to photograph,
and its name to screw on
bumpers and sterns, in their
mania for diversion the almost-rich
air their privacies with skylights,

knock out walls and ceilings
for hand-adzed beams
and hook-scarf joints: whitewashed
inside and out, a few more
authentic capes improve into
our century.

From this harbor the streets tend
toward, craft so elegant we'd wake
bankrupt just for dreaming them
have been drawn up rails
to sleep insectlike in yards
of fitted counterpanes, or spread
sails now among the Antilles.

Only the blunt-bowed draggers
remain, sea trucks built for
the heaping of years on deck,
for troughs they home through
thumping like echocardiograms.

Over locally favored pine-green,
the *Kaiser Bill* and *Old Glory,*
old when I was a boy, have kept
their names as their deep hulls
keep the sea-determined shape
that says this is the way it
has to be for balance
at the culling boards, for yellow
slickers on this gray midwinter water.

Seeing for Ourselves

town dump

There are people so big in the brain
they can't find anything,
the dumpkeeper believes,
and he won't help, so whatever
you see you'll have to see
for yourself. Conditioned by the logo,
don't look for a senatorial mane
or a jaundiced eye, lethally alert.
Gulls will part the air, given
time enough, and head east
and west on sudden errands.
Down that corridor, with the same
black matter-of-fact as crowflight,
only bigger and mottled underneath,
and raggedy the way things
always turn out in home-made
America: one immature bald eagle,
late from a hacking cage,
or with luck and no trace of DDT,
a wild shell. That it looks tired
is only understatement.
It can overtake a pintail,
though it's here for the rats
and a dumped mess of bass.
That it's here at all
is democratic, since we all
come down to this meadow
where the breeze from our overkill
obliterates bloodlines. The dumpkeeper
won't say if he's proud
to be its camarado, just that he
hasn't seen it, but knows if we do
it'll snatch us out of the tanglefoot
of ourselves.

Estuary

Even its latinate carries
water's meander and the release
of rivermouth, as its banks
carry toward dissolution
the tree ideograms and ogham
of gulls, where small scallops
wash up in late December. Snow
in the offing, white-patched
buffleheads flash in the low sun;
eiders who strung their long
black coastwise lines offshore
are gone, and there on the sea-line
between Wood End and the canal,
now there, one at a time,
not workboats looming and fading,
not gray, but black, blackness
asserted without atmospheric
compromise. Then in that
gray under the southerly sun,
a spout, strong, falling in time
away, and a thickening
drawn-out black dash—fin
just before the dive: finbacks,
the pod revealing itself
in breath tree, fin, roll,
piecemeal the way this
one place in the ceaseless
round of the world
offers itself, even when only gulls
might have held cold concourse
on that bar in the estuary.

One for the Lifelist

Not a yellowthroat,
not a yellow warbler, but a
yellow-throated warbler—
it has happened again: the sky
moving out of the west
and before the clouds
migrants come scudding,
so many so fast that the pines
are mobile with blue backs
and bay breasts switching places,
undertail coverts flicking
yellow, white, twitching among
branches, impossible to locate
fast enough, but as though
at the end of summer
an East European primitivist
had painted a Christmas tree
whimsical with birds.
A yellow-throated warbler, one
for the lifelist, though
I promised myself again
I'd swear off this year.
Instead I've come back
for just one more, a failed
teetotaler of birds,
and better this stupefaction at
a lemon-bibbed ounce of
feathers than the shoddy
illusion of the aloneness
of things, wherein the sky
pours down oceanic emptiness
and the life of a grove migrates
across the road to the gas pumps:
even the common foreground
chickadee and background crow
give dimension to our days,
and not to salute such
charity of song

though it be plain as
thumbsqueaks on clear windowpanes,
not to say their names,
and the shadow of death passes
across our tongues.

Below the Hill of the Three Churches

The little oyster dragger swings out
on its hawser as far right
as the first flat run of tide in the channel
allows. It panics a frieze of willets into
running left away from its hull, or else
the hull is still and the shifting birds
suggest motion to it, as a ship departing
will seem to set the pier under way; but now
the dragger's tending left where a
smoke-light skein of least sandpipers
just landed, a shoal creeping forward as
the willets step right, stiff-legged,
mimicking that bridge crossing mud on stilts
far down where a gull begins to slide
on a crawl of heat among exposed hummocks.
Taken with its own effortless riding, it
spins this way on the silt-lift, now that.
Come quick out the door of the Feed and
Grain and ground me with a sack of
sunflower seeds: under three spires
I'd believed rigid until now,
everything's deviating from the mean.

The Patience of White Birches

Because they come up
among others, shyly
among thin oaks and maples
in old fields they're
taking back, we barely
see them. It is only
on lawns of farmhouses
saved from failure
by aluminum coats
colored Swiss Peach or
Brownbread that we
notice their ornamental
docility, how they
stir among themselves,
and on drive-in aprons
where rust has worked
across the screen,
how they seem to stand
at ease, awaiting whatever
voice can crackle
a movie speaker back to
life and stiffen their
spines with marching
orders. Last night
in the Berkshires, they
leaned way over the
highway, looking whitefaced
down into the falling rock
zones, and off in the dark
stood like hairline
faults of frost
driven through stone, nodding
among themselves, seeming
to say, Not by peeling
for canoes ever again,
but by rocks kicked into
gorges one at a time,
by learning the patience of
rust: soon it may take
only one spring.

Apple Talk

I knew in April that would be
the year. Just before time,
all her notice was tuned
to the sky, and she flowered so
you'd blush to put a finger
in among those feelers
Vincent Kay's bees were working.
A shy bearer, and the meat
smells like squashbug, but it'll
pluck your strings all right.
You won't see the gist of this one
vanishing in a supermarket
mirror. One day a grackle flew
into those leaves and came out
a waterthrush, and crossing through
one night from Horton's,
I took her off the breeze
way before I drew near.
The strong ones work some art
of their own. You find them
sometimes still, up away
from here, originals, all scrub
and thorn, set out among
the hardwoods as if by
a sleepwalker. This one I've
christened a Gwaltney Possum:
you take your Gwaltney-Corbin,
it's mush in the flesh
and some worm-prone, too,
but you splice a scion to an
Orr's Possum-nose stock
and you can pitch this fruit
at Wade Boggs, it's that
thick in the hide for wintering
over, and won't let go
your teeth till February.

If Memory Comes to the Tongue

1

I ate a wild one off a cane
by the banks of the Little Pamet,
and now I'm nine miles away
and about that many years old,
somewhere between two pinewood-singing
catbirds on the path from home,
a hot nickel in my hand
I earned picking blackberries.
Once I cross where cicadas
are burning their acetylene and
the sun's unbroken on sand,
Baumgartner will ask
again if I keep my money
in the furnace, and sell me
Lifesavers. If memory
comes to the tongue, maybe
a peppermint will convene
Baumgartner's lost face—or a bowl
of cornflakes, since he seemed
to stock nothing else on
the shelves of his yellow store.

2

Tagged as it was
with a single yellow leaf
like the idea of fall,
green underneath
where the grass wished for it,
and spotted all over with some
apple neurosis from
its tugging between dirt
and sky, maybe it wasn't pretty enough,
but we don't taste with
the eyes, and that one true fruit
in twenty years—
from the top of a tree
we planted among pines—

had outhung the frost, and those
worm-worried on the ground, and that
first apple ever,
which must have wanted
the sharpness
our steel blade elicited from
a sugar ring like
a fully remembered kiss on flesh
clear as heartwood and white flower.

Swallows

1 May

The only one
on this pond, all the rest
a flock composed of
her shadow and
her image on water

and, look, her other
shadow on sand
under water, away from
the black-leaf bottom
that's like so many
more swallows

she appears
to arrive at the far
leaf-shadowed end
before she's quite
left this end, revolving,
speeding the water,

her breeze notching
the chop to blue-black
wingtips, hurrying the pond
through its skinny
flume all morning.

2 October

All that year after we drumrolled
a chopping block over this deck
against the storm door
and went to live inland,
you dreamed weather backing around
east, blindsiding this coast,
howling and driving five hundred
feet of freighter onto
the continental doorstep.
We moved back here for that,

and for October days like this,
when you lead me out
for swallows plummeting
from an eastbound cloud. Now
they pump flukes and hang
high over the house, tippling at
silence that builds toward evening,
and still other swallows
like anchors dragged along
bottomless air try to arrest
the flow of things,
a gathering we wouldn't call
a flock yet. Soon they'll form
and head out over water,
but for now each pump and glide
builds to a letting-go
and tumbling-down to open
restorative wings. If a wren
pokes from a hanging strawberry plant
or a rubythroat stands
in the airborne silhouette
of a seahorse, you see it first.
It's like that day last April when,
watched from another side
of the creation, before sun flashed
on its rubbery head
in barely sliding surf
you knew the seal was there.
There's something between you
and that water, more to you
than I know: your ranges and habitats,
your latitudes and tides
no field guide can delineate.

Rained Out

That wide bay rippled with just
breeze enough, our tacking a mere tilted
luff of sails, and we circled
dolphins all afternoon, two in tandem,
or they circled us, always gone
just so long we'd seance-rap
the hull, and give up, then
five feet off the port side, fin-wheeling
or blowing in our wake, they'd show,
always in the least, last over-the-shoulder
place, eluding all suggestions
of a watery corral, tail-dancing
a half-mile off, sea hams bringing
again and again the gift
of their curiosity, humoring our own
under slow clouds piled white toward
the sun and deepening blue
where they faced oncoming evening,
with clusters of flight here and there,
first August signs of pre-flocks
forming up, and that one broad
underbelly of cloud over
Great Island and the Gut, gray, hairy,
taking its time, looking like something
you might find on the floor beneath
a long-standing frigidaire, then,
over us, letting go not rain
exactly, but fat, single,
ringing drops you could walk between
if you could walk on water,
each with its own pitch, fingerbells
on a delicate Asian hand,
gracenotes on the tide, lasting only
the moment such things can, passing on
toward headlands and the world
of evening light falling into
the harbor's stand of masts,
and the dolphins: gone.

A Cold Bell Ringing in the East

It woke me to this full moon
just pulling away
from the skylight's pine,
and fire in the stove's window
faint as two owls courting
somewhere in these empty woods.
Was it the cold I let in
when I let the dog out
that reduced everything to images,
stripping the rags off ego
and abstraction, shivering
the shadows of the pines?
In this light all our attempts
at this or that mean nothing,
we live by understanding less
than there is in the nose
of this dog construing the air.
That pine is no inn,
the moon's no Chinese courtesan
departing from it a thousand
years ago, and I am not Li Po.
There are those who envy that stone
its decoder-ring luminosity, and those
who would sell the tree.
What joy in having been at all,
in feeding the fire and knowing
that everything isn't about us.
Who can witness these moments
and edges otherwise, except someone
outside them, without
the camouflage of a horned lark,
and praise the virtues of scrub pines
with guardian shapes of sky
among them on these hills?
Only someone not woven into
that fabric, with no protective
coloring, who sees where a deer
is first air, then color of dusk
in scrub, then dusk itself,
with its air of invisible mending.

Wild Blackberries

There are places where things
tie a knot between seasons—
back of fern beds, for instance,
against a steepness
of trees, places you watch
your step, risking ticks,
snakes, maybe tentacles of
something escaped
or paroled from the mind
as too difficult to manage.
Here, for instance (I will not
tell you where), you taste
and look both ways, each bleb
a sweet completion and tart
finality, a trap for
solstice light, a lamp
down hollow, faint in early dark.

Pococurante

Word for the ringsnake
I found in a burl
just under the woodpile tarp,
folded like a black mat of
witches' butter fungus,
trying to shunt itself
its own failing heat, asleep,
so I worked around it,
splitting the pile and facing
the open sides up elsewhere
until, a foot long, longer,
snake poured itself through
itself, down one layer, showing
a yellow collar, and curled
again between two rounds,
buried its head, pococurante,
caring little, like a
stove-settled dog, and as its
tenements disappeared
with the afternoon, spilled
down oak, layer by layer, all
the way to damp earth,
where, discombobulous, it rolled
and stiffened, yellow belly
up, one of those gimp
lanyards woven in childhood,
and I made it a teepee of
bark sleeves to withdraw
from October in, and went away.

For a Daughter Gone Away

Today there've been moments
the earth falters and almost
goes off in those trails of smoke
that resolve to flocks so far
and small they elude my naming.
Walking the old Boston & Maine
roadbed, September, I understand
why it takes fourteen
cormorants to hold the bay's
rocks down. Have I told you
anything you ought to know?
In time you'll come to learn
that all clichés are true, that
a son's a son till he marries,
and a daughter's a daughter
all her life, but today
I want to begin Latin 1 with you
again, or the multiplication
tables. For that first phrase of
unwavering soprano that came
once from your room, I'd suffer
a year of heavy metal. Let all
who believe they're ready for
today call this sentimentality,
but I want the indelible
print of a small hand
on the knees of my chinos again,
now that my head's full of
these cinders and clinkers
that refused fire's refinements.
I wish I could split myself
to deepen and hold on as
these crossties have, and admit
goatsbeard and chicory,
bluecurls and blazing star,
these weeds of your never quite
coming back. I wish I could stop
whatever's driving those flocks
and drove the B & M freights into air.

Getting Through

a little disquisition for my daughter

In one of my dreams somebody
in a white apron's always
yelling, "Come back, you beatnik,"
as I slam out of there just
in time. Water too hot
for human hands is glissading
over the lip of a sink,
or a manager in a paper hat
is threatening, "You don't want
to leave here with a bad taste
in your mouth." Always
the place is hanging over
a mudslide, the river out back
is rising toward warped 2 × 4s,
and I've just said the magic words.
Let the bosses wrestle the sparking
wire or the customer who has to say
the horsemeat's for his dog
every time. How pure a moment
that first one on the pavement.
Even in dreams I breathe original air.
There's a car full of girls and beer
and we're off to the Cape
in a May dusk. That's the ticket
all right, but the ride has to lead
to the place called Sunday evening,
where the fun implodes like
a morning glory: work is the father
of gravity, so whatever went up
comes back down on the ground
in sensible shoes. Cerebral pickpockets
who hustle The Dignity of Labor
never busted a table or tossed
a caesar's salad under the noses
of shrinks on vacation, as you have,
and too much of our time on the planet
is spent discovering things
we don't want to do for too long.

Nevertheless, we arrive by subtraction,
the way a sculptor knocks stone away
until Crazy Horse and his pony
lean into the pure breeze of intention.

The Portuguese Uncle

There was a grove next door
where we scuffed pine needles
to floor plans for other houses
with no wars over groceries, no
maiden aunts penumbral
with desertion, and no grownups
whose remarks to us
nearly disguised their alternate
meanings. Otherwise, we sat
failing on the kitchen steps,
or smoked a hardball through
the morning glories
until Uncle Manny herded us
to his beetle-backed Studebaker
and we drove into his country,
its high smell of fish
snapping us out of it. In rooms
above the wharves talk exploded
in both languages, the one for
cursing hard paymasters
in front of children, the other
for saying the cod went north
and weren't coming back, things
illustrated by hands scored
with the drag of halibut
on droplines. We nursed orange
or grape drinks at enameled
tables, the men sun-browned in
red shirts, with matadors'
smooth hair and noses you tried
not to look at, hands folded
for bottomless silences, in which
to count gulls kiting past
the windows. Once our uncle
yelled, "Popeye!" and there he was,
the anchor cap, the squint,
his corncob in that loaf of chin—
at the door of the plant where

women ripped out orange spawn
and dropped it to the floor,
where trawlers sidling to the wharf
shook the world's tin roof
and spiles and at the scales
lumpers and crews might erupt
out of nothing over prices, where
noon-shriek drove those women
arching in their clothes
one by one to the rainbowed water
we'd dare to enter ourselves, sometime,
we said later, alone, and splash
and kick and swim among them
when they came up, lipstick redder,
hair pasted black, wet
to their true shapes.

Raiding the Boundary Stone

When Mother set out in the dark
with her shovel, our father
would study the ceiling
a serious minute, then dive
back into his paper. There was
something deeper than custom
in this, something like a light
going on in one of the darker
reaches of a chromosome
carried over from Ulster,
the translation of a cattle raid
across water, to where
there were no pastures and no
cows. We could picture
the same scene, one house
up the road. The previous night
and the one after this, Aunt
Ruthie grabbing her spade
by the throat and leaving
for the pillar of cement
that marked the end of the line
two sisters drew. The quick
strike at the border, and soon
paths visible from both houses
to sneaker prints in fresh sand
around the stone, revenge exalted
to an art form that perplexed
the Yankee neighbors,
who'd never seen the Irish
trying to get a purchase on
the New World like this before.
Who knew where it began,
in two little girls elbowing
over the same linoleum square?
One night, late, I cornered
a housebreaker with, "Come out or
I'm coming in," and flushed

Aunt Ruthie from a clump
of scrub pines. This time she
didn't ask if I'd seen her cat,
just stood forgetting where, why.

Against Genealogy

Discovering the provenance of the name,
he marvels again at what fidelity
the genes exact, and wonders if
the dismissal of the Lamarckians
wasn't premature. *From the deep fiord land,*
and the name slides south like an icecap
freighting stones, thistles, and seawater
down the western littoral: Norway,
Scotland, Ulster. First a dollop of
ice for the blood: those glints
at the eyes whenever the salt spray
of a remark is flung after the opening
broadsword cut. Then sawtooth leaves
and spiny discomfort for
the family flower, and poetry drowned
on some twelfth-century North Channel
crossing, but a smatter of economic theory
saved, and added to upon their stony
proximity to Calvinism, so that even
before the Atlantic venture
they are teetotaling on moral
seesaws between the ditches and the stars.
Which brings us to Aunt Delia,
her memoranda to herself in shorthand
above deadbolts, on the refrigerator,
stove, begonia pot, and bathroom mirror
as cryptic to him as runes, and hers to him
Don't touch! Don't eat! as though
the nephew monster's greening—his wrists
and ankles shooting from their cuffs—
could be kept at bay with plain English
until he discovers her one evening
coming down the hill behind the house
with the same gait she used in life
to descend Reed Avenue from business,
armed to the teeth with her own
vigilance, and conflated now with Blackie,
utterly wary and the perfect mouser.

Uncle Patrick and the Doppelgängers

From speculating that the cause
might be something Castro had sprayed
on the wrapper of his Havana cigar,
he switched to considering mirages,
oceanic inversions of the air
that can hang a ship on a sky,

and there on O'Connell Street
may have projected his own image
transatlantic, far from the library
in Massachusetts where he regularly
saved the lives of children
by throwing out the latest Rod McKuen.

But wasn't he here already?
From Eason's doorway he watched himself
pass out of sight in that crowd, their faces
still reflecting the weather of fields
in that city of the instant retort.

I always had the mug for agriculture,
he thought, and said it aloud days later
on the Sky Road, while wind edged
the rental car toward a wave of horned heads
dividing at his fenders,

and beyond the last haunch, bobbling around
among the wiper's passes, his plainly
confused face, which—when the cattle passed
and he got out to examine shattered
side mirrors and gouged paint—

was nowhere in sight. Me, or my obsession
with myself, driven to the edge by
atmospheric conditions? Am I dead, or just
doggedly coercing the elements?

He considered the likelihood of chance
encounters with all his manifestations:

profiled in pubs; thumping a guitar
outside Kilkenny Castle, his foot working
the machinery of a tap-dancing duck.

What a face apt for stone, he whispered later
in that leaf maze accented by the birds:
a Hibernio-Romanesque doorway, and above the arch,
stacked like grocers' cabbages, a pyramid
of heads, all of them his.

But now imagine him again as a bishop.
Though of course, he thought, I always had
that nose battered as though from
theological scrimmaging, and even in high school
the requisite five o'clock shadow which,

at convocations, makes bishops look like Cosa Nostra
gathered for the team picture: Uncle Patrick
croziered and mitered, a stone rocket
waiting to be shot whistling to heaven,
meanwhile leaning in a two-fingered blessing
to himself from a niche in a Sligo church wall.

You Drove Out from Drogheda

Once, on a dare, you stuck a fist
in that scummed well by the ruined
abbey graveyard—such steel
at your pulse that something
deep under seemed to lock onto
your wrist. Uneasy because the earth
proves the depths that ask something
of you, that light has to fall
across such distances from the sun,
on Saint John's Eve you won't
leap the flames anymore, but smirk
behind a beer at any girl
superstitious enough to circle
the bonfire three times for a lucky
wedding, and children bearing lit
sticks of it homeward like tapers.
You drove out from Drogheda last night
to a field above here,
where work on the new gas line
was brought up short—
skeletons that carbon-dated back
fourteen centuries. Word of
those bones had gotten onto Boyneside
Radio, and the first line of defense
when you can't prevent last night
from loitering in your head
will be the dope a foreign sailor
ferried up the chemical Boyne
and sold you, or some concoction of
boredom, Smithwick's Ale, and hormones.
You broke six skulls, but the stone
heads that keep breaking through
Irish clay won't be kept down.
Their noses, battered with having been
places, want to go on; their crossed eyes
are unreasonable about what their mouths
appear to be shouting at you.

Cuckoo

A bull of sorrowful eye
who'd learned to negotiate
the bedspring rigged
to keep him on the grazing
near Labbamolaga,

one grandmother pushing
another up my lane
of the N4
in a wheelchair,

and a man crouched,
gnawing and hollow-eyed,
in the sun at the second
recess of a bridge
over the Garavogue:

in Ireland I learned
to keep in mind
that whatever I might
imagine might be there
on the far left side
of all bends anywhere,

learned to think cat
or stoat on every corner,
whatever could part
the ditchgrass and vanish,
never Jack Russell terrier
trotting importantly somewhere,

or a man near Ballyvaughn
leading a donkey
ridden by a dog
pretending to be a man
in sunglasses smoking a pipe.

And so, why not you,
the only cuckoo in my life,
calling from the bourn
of the fourth dimension

at Corcomroe, a place I loved
for its name alone—
before I ever saw
Conor O'Brien sleeping
in effigy by the abbey wall,
a king his swordless
stone made simple,

watched over by stone faces
with lidded eyes, that didn't
sneer or smile above
the tribes and loyalties
crossed on those fields
and gone like the turloughs'
transient pools.

When I dropped through the colors
of summer evening, changes
the limestone took
and parted with on hills
out a window, deepening into
stony sleep myself,

you were trying over and over
to say Corcomroe, and I woke
to morning and you again,
among gentians the glacier
had dragged from Italy
and Arctic avens
it had pushed south and seeded
in those limestone clefts

where you were slipping
off through the leaves, less
and less Corcomroe's counterweight,
hunting that other syllable
you would always need
to name the place.

Anchorites

1 On the Saints' Road

Pilgrim again, over those ancient
cattle tracks pressed into service
as national highways, wherever
the Guide to Ireland inflated
a vestige of half-buried stones
to a saint's tale, or injected
the least trickle with miracles,
I picked my way through
a glossary of belief: Reask,
Kilmalkedar, Labbamolaga. While the wind
piled rain on the stones, my spirit
stumbled and crashed about in its
puffin mask like someone at a party
coming unglued, sick of benign
explanations for everything
under the sun. I wanted beyond craving
some wonder and mystery
mortared with crushed shells, horsehair,
milk, and feculence, some blunt
and basic anchorite
with the cold-boned authority
eras of Atlantic weather convey
to step round-eyed
from his stone and beat hell
and humanism out of me,
screaming, "This is the way!"
It never happens, of course. But
once, home a week, passing
the John Hancock Tower, my unforgetting
cochlea released across evening fields
a West Country cuckoo call, an answer
of sorts, and I crouched
to the sidewalk, expecting a hail of glass.

2 Reply to a Saint Patrick's Day Card

Shamrocks he demonstrated the Trinity
through, they ate. Robed and barbered,
touched with the airbrush, he looks
incapable of stepping ashore somewhere
far down the Rhine and busting up
the local idols with an oar,
or sailing to Iceland's penitential
freeze for the crime of knocking
another bishop down
when a small theological point
turned physical. But in all
the looks and acts of those anchorites,
as in their armpits, there was
more than a touch of the goat:
they could blister cheeks with a curse
or go years without a word,
fearing nothing but the day the sky
might fall on them, and with all
the goat-minded insouciance of art,
carved the name of their savior
in fish-shape on obstructions
to ocean where no one
would want to live but them,
and there prayed so hard
that body-light splayed through
unmortared walls. Given
a minute, they ask too much
of us. Therefore no holidays for them.

West Cork: The Road Bowlers

On one leg, arms held open to the sky
like some leftover anchorite
praying in a stream, he's in
the middle of this road
to Cahermore, body-steering
his steel ball through its arc,
a local champ who sidesteps
our fender as we pass with care
between the dapper gauntlet of men
fresh-suited from Mass this Sunday.
They seem more familiar
than those waiting for the tanker
a weekday morning, by silvery urns
steaming with heat of udders
where three roads cross at a sky-blue
store. Eyes lit for the genial crack,
today they are starched
to their ruddy chins and face by face
repopulate a Massachusetts
crowd from memory. Here's someone
who might tell you a story
beginning, Long ago at the morning
of the world . . . And here's a godfather,
at least two monsignors, companions
from grade school grown up,
and several philosophers
of the funeral parlor, these open,
generous faces again. The wind
bowing that one-string fence
more keenly, drawing clouds eastward
over this Beara Peninsula,
has thrown emigration into reverse,
and that sea managing seven weathers
goes gray. But now they are smiling
and waving us past as if to say,
Safe journey and no fear. As if
it is all as simple as their pastime:
the road and ball, the finish line.
As if from here to there
is only a clamber over this pasture wall.

The Stones of Callanish

Outer Hebrides

So far removed from bishops
of dressed stone, from detailed
miter and slippers, from green men
on the tympana of churches,
whose mouths discourse
in dialects of leaves,

these seem the stone equivalent
of a grove, set here by those
who missed the mainland oaks
where once they huddled under boughs
that muttered phrases out.

But here's a shoulder,
there's a hip outthrust.
This crowd is social: over there
the chest of some hero
almost starting through,
and here's the necessary womb curve.

Tall and narrow, some look almost
reasonable, elders explaining
to a folk whose faces seem mis-hung
and woebedogged.

Down the island at Rodel Church
you see the next step,
and over the water at Moone Cross:
whole figures barely released
from the mineral, almost tricks of light,

no more detailed than gingerbread men—
except the eyes, which bug as though
astonished at this world, their vision
never to be reined by fiat or commandment.

Crossing Pentland Firth

"We might not see the Old Man of Hoy
this time. They climbed it
on American TV," somebody says,
then beats it for the stern, hand
over mouth. Trough and wave, I step
around in most surprising ways.
Glasses jig on tables; quite at random
doors open and close, but no one's
passing through. The ferry
nosedives like a submarine. Its fake
wood panels flex and squeal like rats
weeping to desert. Maybe the Brit
quizmaster on the tube has tipped
these sleepers toward chlorotic naps.
Buckets of buckshot spray, wave
and trough. Finnbarr, Ninian, Columba,
old sea saints bobbing in your nutshells
on this gannet road, I cannot
picture you this way. Was there
seasickness when the hand of faith
lay open under everything, with even
Greenland barely a dare among you?
We're ill, moderns praying for
guillemots to show up and foreshadow
Orkney houses that will break
in a gray wave on our eyes.

Noss

In yellow solipsist faces
the gannets stand around
on their slabs like Hyde Park cranks
orating to themselves in every
direction. Guillemots
shuffle for position, their formal
stag lines ledged on the cliff walls—
too much life and nothing that wants
you here on this island where humans
have thrived less than trees.
At the point called Mansie's Berg
someone lived once, and Norsemen
named this bay Rumble Wick.
Walls the Shetland wrens flit
in and out of, feeding their young,
were laid a stone at a time
across this woolpatch texture of
peat, rock, sheep scat, wind,
and ocean sun—moorlands where
the new lambs bleat under cover
of eroded gullies, where fulmars
nesting on the edge
work their bull necks for offensive
oils when you come too near.
Solstice, and druids on Income
Support convene at Stonehenge,
mobilizing the police, but here
there are no fire-eaters
or jugglers, only kittiwakes
cruising your steps, then great
skuas coming in low enough
to rap your skull
with a fisted claw. Even the mild
wheatears seem outraged
at your stumbling on this mad
bird-birthing place of
the universe. It is all cackling,
whines, mewlings against

your presence, until one of
the meanings of islands
where the final hangers-on
petitioned for removal dawns on you,
and now you have a little litany
which goes, Noss, Taransay, Scarp,
Mousa, St. Kilda, to support you
toward some measure of humility.

Norwegians at the Shetland Hotel

Fifty years ago, sailing home on one cylinder
every chance they got, into head seas
and maybe the Luftwaffe, explosives
or saboteurs under a layer of fish or peat
in the holds of those widow-makers
that had brought them here across the North Sea,
they would slip into a local fleet after dark,
then up a fiord toward a contact or quisling
or the Gestapo, and if sunk or found out
swam for it, arrived snowblind at the doors
of strangers, found "the Shetland Bus,"
and sailed west to report back here and sail
eastward home again to help tie up ten German
divisions. Last night in the hotel,
pink and popeyed as a gang of trolls
some burial mound disgorged, bemedaled and drunk,
trying to walk the walls and ceilings, in every
sense defying gravity, they woke me late
and early, singing something Norse on the roads
and in the corridors, marching as surely
out of step as in 1942, a matter of
principle then as now. Old heroes
dwarfed by the docked steel of floating
factories out of the Black Sea and Faeroe,
they revived long-faced for noon, the descent
of Eric Bloodaxe, and followed beflowered wives
up the gangplank of the Bergen ferry.

Far Mulliskay

If the soul leaves the body as a mouse,
as once they believed here,
and the island house-mice were extinct
a year from the removal,
what is this wraith-rustle

dogging my steps in the grass,
stopping when I stop? Someone the lark's
trying to explain, as it scales
the long and short of its Morse code
too fast for me to follow?

The Free Kirk preacher, perhaps,
still in his mad-hatter getup
that established primacy over barefoot Celts
even before two languages collided
as surely as this lark's and mine,

the reverend's karma to remain here,
waylaying island-addicts like me,
forced to account to their backs
for sheepdogs that bloated in the bay,
dragging stones because there'd be
no work for them after the dispersal?

A hazard of loose roof slates, his manse
oversees this thatchless village yet,
this huddle of close walls
that goes on betraying dependence.

Newly tubercular, prone now to money
and clocks, from the outposts of their diaspora
the islanders would swear they were happy
here under force eight winds,
where nothing grew taller than themselves.

Where they went they tended to move
toward the miracle of a moving

automobile, as though danger related
only to wind and water, places
where four waves meeting
could suck down a boat.

Now a lapwing takes up the story,
patroll ing close while I wander
dry-stone mazes that enclosed families
with cattle, a design translated to
the Great Plains sodhouse. She flies
as far as the outlines of old crop strips—

oats, rye, potatoes—then draws her circle
tighter when I enter the graveyard
where her brood must huddle
in a scrape of earth. A femur, broken
crosses, a set of quernstones
barely improved from a Pictish grain mill.

Belief can be worse than the weather: the children
in old age wouldn't remember singing
except in six hours of Sunday church
and at daily services

when they should have been hunting eggs
and salting down gannets for winter,
good works and a form of prayer that stood
the islanders well two thousand years.

Mist builds its mountain above the mountain.
Summering ewes scramble higher. Not enough
nimble men to rope each other in teams
and harvest the birds from cliff faces

and the old scattered oats on their tables
and opened the Gaelic Bible to Exodus.
Across the water Glasgow waited,
lit like Saturday night in hell.

Sky and Island Light

"My mother used to watch the angels
diving off the clouds up there.
They'd fly back up, climb on,
and dive again like boys
swimming off the rocks those few
hot afternoons in July. And why not,
Saint Michael and them, so serious
in their work? They need such play."

St. Finnbarr's Cemetery, Barra,
sky and island light, and Mrs. MacNeill
running a wire brush over the stones
of her mother and father. Three chapels'
dry-stone traces, but no roof for
an agoraphobe. I studied the edges
of a cloud building cauliflower shapes
higher. Slants of sun as from
an alien machine were probing the waters
by Eriskay. The young, as always,
were leaving for the cities.
                                        "They'll
not see any angels in Edinburgh,"
she said. "The island gives you a right
relation to yourself. You're small
but you're not lost in the dimensions
of the place you know. I suppose
if you're tired of seeing angels,
you're tired of everything."
                                        She nodded
at her mother's stone. "That's what
she said before she passed over,
I'm tired of waiting for those angels.
All I can do is keep the moss off them,
and if I've strength enough, sometimes
I'll give the in-laws a scrub, too."

Under My Stornoway Hat

Thinking along its designs
that look like the mingled sea routes
of wandering Picts, Celts,
and Norsemen, mumbling the names
of their ports, I see how Scalloway
might render to scallawag,

how all my life, hanging around
harbors, three sheets to the wind
on their air of departures alone—
roadstead, outward bound,
hull down for anywhere, a lingo
that lifts my nape hairs—

I might have become a seaport's
drunk if poems hadn't
grabbed me by the throat.
If I say Caledonian-MacBrayne,
my pulse rate drops and I'm ready
to sail on just my name

for Stromness or Lerwick or Ullapool,
anywhere oystercatchers and lapwings
stand in for lowly pigeons,
places precipitated onto the sea-line
because they're too blue
for the sky, lumps of holy island
blue as the wool of this hat,
that now and again disappear

and return with more curlews
in a single field than I've counted
in a lifetime. Here in this livingroom,
in this magical blue hat, I see
how Stornoway commends itself
to stowaways, and this sheep-smelling
wool recalls the Soay ram
who told me, side-of-his-mouth
near Scrabster, Keep moving.